PIANO · VOCAL · GUITAR

# THIS IS US

## SELECTIONS FROM THE SERIES SOUNDTRACK

ISBN 978-1-5400-2782-5

Visit Hal Leonard Online at
**www.halleonard.com**

Contact Us:
**Hal Leonard**
7777 West Bluemound Road
Milwaukee, WI 53213
Email: info@halleonard.com

In Europe contact:
**Hal Leonard Europe Limited**
Distribution Centre, Newmarket Road
Bury St Edmunds, Suffolk, IP33 3YB
Email: info@halleonardeurope.com

In Australia contact:
**Hal Leonard Australia Pty. Ltd.**
4 Lentara Court
Cheltenham, Victoria, 3192 Australia
Email: info@halleonard.com.au

# BEAUTY AND PAIN

Words and Music by
PAUL HOFFMAN

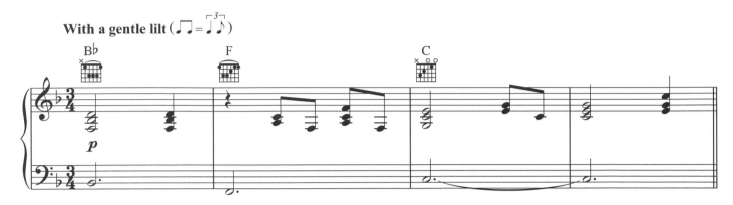

Please take the words _____ to car-ry a-way. _____ There's

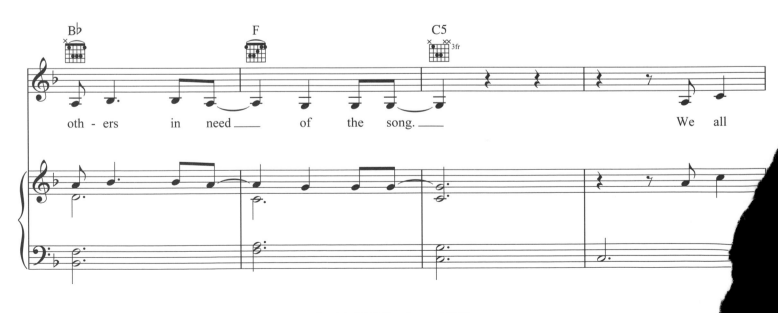

oth-ers in need _____ of the song. _____ We all

# CAN'T FIND MY WAY HOME

Words and Music by
STEVE WINWOOD

# COME TALK TO ME

Words and Music by
PETER GABRIEL

# IF ONLY

Words and Music by
MARIA TAYLOR

# WATCH ME

Words and Music by
LABI SIFFRE

Watch me when ___ you look ___ my way,          see me smil -
Watch me when ___ I'm on ___ my own,          see me fall -

- ing,          be my night ___ and day.
- ing          like the snow.

Touch me in ___ your own ___ sweet way, ___          feel me trem -
Come and be ___ the things ___ you are, ___          I'm still fall -

# WE CAN ALWAYS COME BACK TO THIS

Words and Music by SIDDHARTHA KHOSLA
and RICHARD PIERCE

# WHERE DO THE CHILDREN PLAY

Words and Music by
YUSUF ISLAM

# WITHOUT YOU

Words and Music by PETER HAM
and THOMAS EVANS

*\* Recorded a half-step higher*

# WILLIN'

Words and Music by
LOWELL GEORGE

**Country Ballad**

warped by the rain, ___ driv-en by the snow. I'm drunk and dirt-y, don't you know? But I'm
kicked by the wind, ___ robbed by the sea, had my head stove in ___ but I'm still on my feet, ___ and I'm

still                will-ing.
still                will-ing.                                              Now, I

B/D#

Out on the road ____ late last night, I've seen ____
smug - gled some smokes ____ and folks from Mex - i - co, _____

C#m7                B        A

____ my pret - ty Al - ice in ev - 'ry head - light.
Baked     by   the   sun   ev - 'ry   time   I   go   to Mex -

E              A    B    A    E

Al - ice,          Dal - las   Al - ice.}          And I've been from ____
i - co.            Oh, and  I'm  still. __  }

A                    B                              E

Tuc - son   to   Tu - cum - ca - ri,   Te - ha - cha - pi to To - na - pah. ____   Driv - en

will - ing ___ to be mov - ing. ___

D.S. al Coda

# THE WIND

Words and Music by
CAT STEVENS

# THE WORLD IS SMILING NOW

Words and Music by JIM JAMES
and LEONARD E. SANDERS